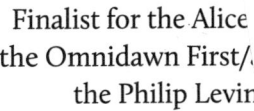

'*Objects from April and May* is an extended meditation on loss, shock and identity that also refuses easy identifications. A moving collection written with love and defiance.'
— Isabella Hammad, author of *The Parisian*

'Heartbreaking and gorgeous, *Objects from April and May* explores the richness of life's fleeting yet monumental moments, where everything is at stake. Zena Agha leads us on a regenerative journey of crossings between the material, the political and the personal.'
— Heba Hayek, author of *Sambac Beneath Unlikely Skies*

'Rich in memory, thought and materiality, Zena Agha's poems are profound psychological experiences, straddling worlds lost to circumstance and war, occupation and geopolitics. *Objects from April and May* shows a serious conviction; a yearning for an alternative version of what is, and an imagining of what's also possible.'
— Anthony Anaxagorou, author of *After the Formalities*

'Zena Agha's poems shape-shift between poetry and prose, word and image, interiority and tabulation, dream and document. She writes in the space between, in her words, state failure and the apocalypse, in an ongoing attempt to inventory what has gone missing: a stolen talisman and the lost homeland that it signified.'
— Ken Chen, author of *Juvenilia*

'A book which feels "materially in the world", whose poems-as-talismans can't be stolen or lost, because they're really alive.'
— Will Harris, author of *RENDANG*

OBJECTS FROM
APRIL AND MAY

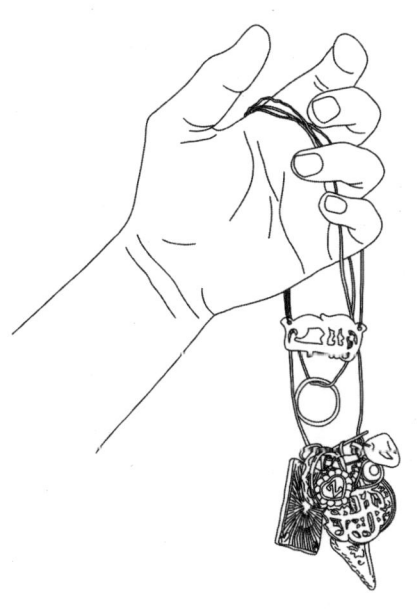

First published in the United Kingdom in 2022
by Hajar Press C.I.C.
www.hajarpress.com
@hajarpress

ISBN 978-1-914221-12-5 Paperback
ISBN 978-1-914221-13-2 EPUB eBook

A Cataloguing-in-Publication data record for this book is available
from the British Library.

Cover and interior art: Hanna Stephens
Cover design: Samara Jundi
Typesetting: Laura Jones / lauraflojo.com

Printed and bound in the United Kingdom by
Clays Ltd, Elcograf S.p.A.

OBJECTS FROM
APRIL AND MAY

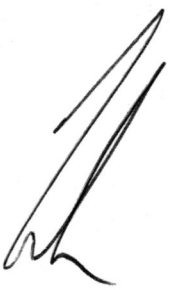

ZENA AGHA

For my mother Jenan
for the gold and everything else

وَمَا الْحَيَاةُ الدُّنْيَا إِلَّا مَتَاعُ الْغُرُورِ

And what is the life of this world except
the enjoyment of delusion

Qur'an 3:185

Contents

AUTHOR'S NOTE

As I write this, my mother's sister, my khala, is in Baghdad. She went to settle a family feud involving inheritance. I've asked her to bring back my things.

In the time before the pandemic, I rented an apartment in the Baghdad Al-Jadeeda neighbourhood of the city and lived in the thumping heart of the market. I had arrived with two suitcases, filled with the beloved and the banal—a hot water bottle, a photograph developed by a far-away friend, a stack of books, a trench coat from upstate New York, academic articles about an ancestor who had dominated northern Palestine in the Ottoman period.

In the first week of March 2020, I flew to London for two speaking engagements and a wedding. I filled a suitcase with the dirty sheets too annoying to wring through the rooftop washing machine and bunches of fresh dates for a friend. The day of my return flight, Iraq closed its borders and the UK lurched into a lockdown.

I spent many secluded months contemplating my scattered items and calculated that I had mattresses in Brooklyn, Baghdad and London—and a home in none. I had, despite their cautions, mirrored the estrangement of my parents—in the sense that they left their homes in Iraq and Palestine and have never fully arrived at new ones.

The closest articulation I could find of this liminal state came from the Palestinian poet Mourid Barghouti, who wrote that 'it is enough for a person to go through the first experience of uprooting, to become uprooted forever. It is like slipping on the first step of a staircase. You tumble down to the end.'[1]

As lockdown continued and I tasted the delights of a quiet city and newfound pastimes, I began to wear clothes I had stored away aged seventeen. I came to regard my wardrobe, my bookshelf and the detritus under my bed as an archive of sorts. An imprint of who I was a decade earlier and how she continues to blaze from within me.

Now, my aunt visits the houses of family members to recover my possessions, sorting through the remains of an impossible fire. She has held up t-shirts, towels and annotated books over WhatsApp. One Tuesday evening, she lost her temper and scolded: '*Habibti*, I'm happy to do this, but truthfully, I told your mother you're being difficult. This stuff, most of this means nothing—go to the shops and buy more. Why remember these things?'

*

This isn't a manuscript about that experience, but it is a rumination on lost things and the depths to which we can lose ourselves in tracing them.

1   Mourid Barghouti, *I Saw Ramallah*, trans. Ahdaf Soueif, New York: Anchor Books, 2003, p. 131.

On a balmy Saturday evening in late April 2019, my then partner (now husband) and I were robbed at gunpoint outside his house in Oakland, California. The attackers took three gold necklaces, the most treasured of which—a chain that held charms and pendants—I wore for almost two decades.

The robbery turned violent and, when I think of it now, it ranks as one of those fleeting moments where death is suddenly and inexplicably possible. Where the gossamer-fine curtain between breathing in the world (and enduring its preoccupations) and no longer existing is pulled away.

But when I mourn the incident, the grief isn't for the horror of the moment, nor the pain that came after it. It is almost entirely for the loss of the most precious object I ever knew. In the aftermath, I traced and re-traced every item worn around my neck and realised each was a statement, a fact from some person or place, some impulse or encounter. It felt as though several parts of me were reified in them.

For a period, before I fell asleep, I would invent alternative paths. They ended, in some form or another, with the attackers returning what they had taken. Sometimes with their mother present, sometimes with an apology, but always with an understanding that no more would be said. Not now I had the chains fastened once again around my neck.

In the harshness of the morning, however, I would recall Mourid Barghouti's lament: 'Nothing that is absent

3

ever comes back complete. Nothing is recaptured as it was.'[2] Not my gold, not my homeland.

*

The encounter reminded me that I am materially in the world. I love what the world is made of. The way we make other things from it; how we give and receive parts of it.

It taught me that I love gold. I love its history, its colour, its properties, the way it is malleable yet durable. I love how we anchor ourselves, our religions, our cultures and our aspirations to it. How we court lovers, family and strangers with it. I love how it arrives to me.

Just as we exchange gold for goods, I have exchanged what was torn from me for this work. See this as an offering. A manifesto for the preciousness and precarity of objects.

2 Barghouti, *I Saw Ramallah*, p. 87.

PLAYLIST

Frank Ocean – 'Nights'

Kendrick Lamar feat. Rihanna – 'LOYALTY.'

FKA twigs – 'Two Weeks'

IAMDDB (Prod. Adrian) – 'Quarantine'

Yasmine Hamdan – 'La Ba'den'

Laura Mvula – 'Sing to the Moon'

Ólafur Arnalds – 'Near Light'

SALES – 'Off and On'

Kelis feat. André 3000 – 'Millionaire'

Fadel Chaker – 'Ya Ghayeb'

Jah9 – 'Humble Mi'

William Onyeabor – 'Atomic Bomb'

SUTTER AVENUE/
RUTLAND ROAD

There are people/ on the internet/ that I hold myself up
to/ their success a litmus for mine/ I would be surprised/
if they thought/ of me/ at all.

I feel better/ when I remember/ that humans created it/
all: haute culture, aeroplanes, awards, straight lines.

I read a quote once/ when sorting/ through what notions
/would continue/ into adulthood./ It read/ 'in 100 years,
there'll be all new people'.

And now/ I think of my apartment building/ from 1922/
it is close/ when I remember/ that Mama's bibi was a
woman/ but far/ when I remember/ that everyone/ alive
then/ is mostly dead/ now.

These ideas are freeing/ but also make me/ despondent/
like the first time/ I saw Jupiter/ through the telescope/
at the science centre/ and looked down/ at my silk
trousers/ (the ones Khala bought me/ when she knew/
Mama was upset/ with her)/ and thought/ this all means
nothing.

29TH APRIL

On the second morning, I could not remember if the word 'shadow' was spelt with one or two d's. I had crossed it with the word 'shallow' and passed many anguished moments in thought. Had I closed my eyes, I would have seen the hand—

extended. So I looked obliquely at the light and thought about humankind. How groups form (and whom we remove). The normativity of good and evil. How, in these dusky breaths, only pain feels honest.

Then I sensed the left side of my face—the unbroken part—against the skin of the pillow. I ache all over.

In the pre-dawn drive from Highland, my mother warns I will wake, with hurt spread across my body, like sickness.

She tells me it happened twice to her
like that—she tells me not to worry.

In the months since, my mother and I pass much time discussing the Attack when I was five. The myriad of ways it shattered her life and mine. I thought I knew all there was about shame. She teaches me more.

AN IMPORTANT LESSON IN PRIORITISATION

In Arabic: في مهم وفي أهم

That is to say: *there is that which is important,
and that which is most important.*

It is important
to make a home that pleases me.

This means: dusting leaves,
counting thread, passing salt.

This means: seeing half of your face
from half of mine.

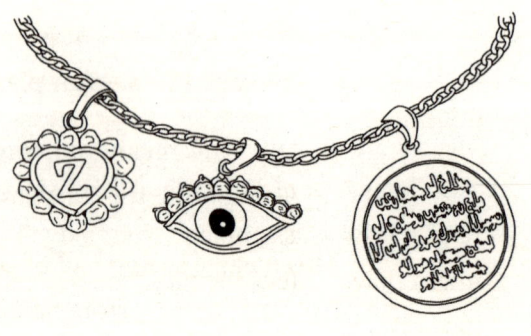

TALISMAN (1)

The first three items on that chain were:

i.　　　Heart-shaped. Kitsch crystals around 'Z'. (00–19)

ii.　　　Open hand in gold. Its palm, evil eye in blue.
　　　　(0?–08) Replaced with the lemon of an eye from
　　　　Mecca. Mama rebuked: Wear it louder. *Lazim*. It
　　　　must claw the evil from every eye that sees you.
　　　　(08–19)

iii.　　　A bulbous *Ayat al-Kursi*. Aged seven, it was the
　　　　reason for the assemblage. You know, I think it
　　　　might (have) be(en) the most precious thing.
　　　　(00–19)

FLIGHT B6 1415

From time to time
I have the urge to change
everything in my life
for the sake of a single object.

When I was younger
a yellow stereo,
last week
a pair of jeans.

Earlier (packing for San Francisco)
I wore them
with a t-shirt shrunk
at the end of summer.

Facing my mirror:
I am gorgeous.

I rarely transform.
To place that hope
on objects alone
requires a reassessment

of all my objects
that includes this body.

Objects of flesh

are impossible to wholly
acquire or discard

and generally
there's a rupture

in the attempt.

GOLD RUSH

99284 emergency room visit level 4 three thousand four hundred and ninety one dollars ~~it~~ J7030 IV Soln 1000Cc'S one hundred and twenty nine dollars ~~is~~ 81025 urine pregnancy test one hundred and seventy dollars ~~expensive~~ 70496 Ct head angiography seven thousand three hundred and fourteen dollars ~~to~~ 70498 Ct neck angiography seven thousand one hundred and four dollars ~~remain~~ 72125 CT C-SPINE WITHOUT CONTRAST four thousand one hundred and sixty one dollars ~~alive~~ 70450 Ct head Wo/Contrast three thousand two hundred and ninety one dollars ~~in~~ 70486 computed tomography, maxillofac three thousand six hundred and forty five dollars Q9967 CONTRAST 300-399 MG P/ML NON-IO six hundred dollars Q9967 CONTRAST 300-399 MG P/ML NON-IO six hundred dollars ~~America~~ commercial other insurance paym zero dollars receivable total thirty thousand five hundred and five dollars grand total thirty thousand five hundred and five dollars ~~but~~

THE MATERIAL INTELLECT AS A DISPOSITION WITH THE SOUL AS SUBJECT

I am changing my sheets. Bella tells me objects
are strange because we personify them. We
are on the phone. Everyone thanks God

I am alive.
No one listens. Without those
objects, shapes, mined from crevices of before,
~~I am less alive~~ since their loss

I am two.
This one, in this body, who eats,
sleeps long hours,
finds company strenuous.
And a lost other.

That makes this one search
old notes on celestial bodies,
souls, intellects, the confrontation between
Al-Ghazali and Ibn Rushd
and other theological and philosophical ideas.

TALISMAN (2)

Other items on that chain were:

iv. A dense imitation of the Qur'an. An amorphous hunger pulled me to the window in Al-Kadhimiya. $60 and some dinars. (04–19)

v. A tooth-sized Nefertiti held by a nail-sized safety pin. (14–19)

vi. A small turtle (21 karat) and a supine hula dancer (9 karat). With the insurance money from the Saab, we fly to Hawaii. Mama will do anything for me. (08–19)

LATE CAPITALISM

still young awake
hear the ocean

in this fugue state
I bend myself

listen to water
rushing then possessive

at Kilburn mosque
a man clarifies:

it is music.
A body is always

disrupted in strange
beds. Crouch outside

those stars frighten,
a canopy of

jewelled eyes, unforgiving
blackness lingers

over crossroads
the way men still hold you

even though you're grown.
This house is filled and

full avocadoes,
mangoes, guavas draw

a papaya as big
as a new-born

from the freezer
reckless, run a lethal

blade through blood orange
and arcane the seeds

like tadpoles fish them
with a spoon, quarter

then quarter again
devour with jackfruit

for breakfast, the skins
a discarded snake

the pips, bullets.
Slow exoticism.

What of their delivery?
Listen: if you are working

because paper makes
you, then fate has left

your life flavourless.

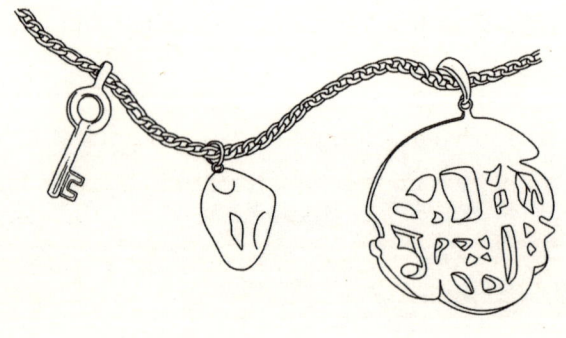

TALISMAN (3)

More items on that chain:

vii. A small key. 'The key to my heart' (Mama). *'Bess kamaan, haqq al-'Awda'* (me). (12?–19)

viii. An amber stone. 'It absorbs negative energy' (Mama). She bows her head, lifts her chain, slides her gift. Like a promise. (12?–19)

ix. A saintly circle fished from a suit pocket. A present my father has no need of. I have been invisible for three Februarys. (12?–19)

DAMASCUS

Even though
    I eat at her table
        only once

I grieve Amma Fajr
    the way empire grieves glory.
        'It is like I am sitting beside my brother.'

Above my eyes
    a sore thrill
        from my form metamorphosing

into his.
    Categorisation as kin
        that does not control.

In writing
    I realise
        this yearning

falls
    mostly
        to him.

Baba as boy
        or blessing
                bewilders.

That war
        swallowed her
                is limiting.

Earlier,
        two
                swallowed him.

I don't dare
        to dive in
                to find him.

OBJECTS FROM THE GOLAN

Age twenty-three

                           only

        he returns
        he collects

furniture. Objects

                         alone

        are spared
        this غربة.

ELEGY FOR RETURN NO. 1

Let me be clear about what I want.
I want return, yes, but more. To turn
stones back. I read once about a
mosque being made into a bar. Now,
I can forgive iconoclasm, but that did
offend. You hate when I talk about
return but some things just have to
be spoken and anyway, my father is
older than you and while he never
spoke it, he was mighty pleased to see
the lemon. I told you it's a kibbutz
now. Off route 90, near where
Jesus fed five thousand. And so, it is
perfectly right that my savage nose
of a father was born near Jesus and
my grandmother turned chairs into
thrones.

MU'ADALA (معادلة)

إذا If

1 is perishing gratefully[1]

و And

10 is Leila, Al-Qassam and any resistance that ever knew arms[2]

إذاً Then

Boycotting, divesting and sanctioning = 3[3]

---

[1] While still not existing

[2] We cannot forgive them for forcing us to kill their children

[3] If (in a capitalist superstructure) one cannot select what dates, printers and soap to buy, then surely one cannot be Free

ELEGY FOR RETURN NO. 2

Everyone says it is about land, but
I believe it is about time. What are
seventy-some years in the grand
kaleidoscope of sunsets? And, if three
thousand years are what is noted,
then certainly every rotation between
that moment and this is noteworthy.

THE ANIMALS AT QALQILIYA ZOO

were mostly tear-gassed
during the second intifada

*

of their being, only
the formal cause remains

*

the *shuhada* taxidermy
with their stuffed gums

*

skin is shape
is outline is deceit

ELEGY FOR RETURN NO. 3

When we are alone, we talk about
return. We all think, 'good, yes!'

عودة in Arabic is more urgent.

One seismic rumble from our throat.
One blast, filling our cheeks. One
tongue, rapping the backs of teeth.
And out, at last! Into this ether. Free.

Then, we all speak, 'tomorrow,
tonight!'

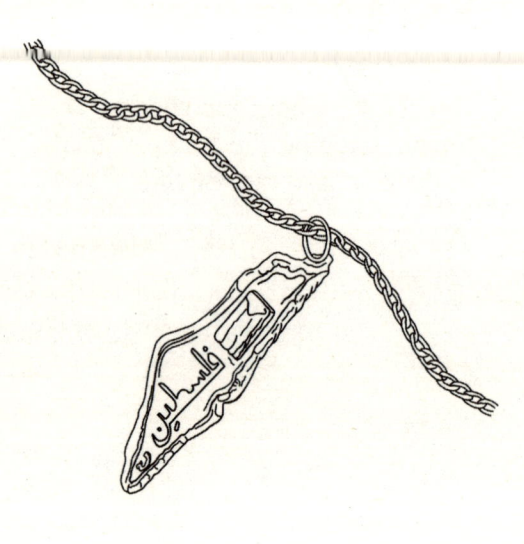

TALISMAN (4)

The changeling on the chain:

x.
A map
of home.
For decades,
it is our secret
battle-cry. Until
one March, I am
detained in Area C.
The Mizrahi soldier
has one, just like mine.
Except, his is hollow
—the star of David
crossing straight
through. Soon,
I will dream
of soldiers
tearing it
from
my
ne-
ck

.

3RD MAY

I revisit photographs
from even a week ago.

That Saturday, I have
two conversations,

both with Arabs.
The first, on Seventeenth

and Telegraph, reads my name.
The second,

in the Mission, reads my name.
Exclaims

he is from Bethlehem.
Between us, a pot

lemongrass
two cups.

He disregards
fi-l-dakhil, bi '48.

He responds
It is all Palestine.

This is the password.
I present the map.

Defiance need not
be dramatic.

At nine o'clock, at closing,
a box of harissa

for us, it is
a poetic goodbye.

IN CASE YOU NEED
DIRECTIONS

from MacArthur BART Station, Oakland, CA 94609
to 985 44th St, Oakland, CA 94608

17 min (0.8 mile) arriving 9.55 p.m.
via 40th St and West St
Mostly flat
Use caution—walking directions may not always reflect
real-world conditions

MacArthur BART Station
Oakland, CA 94609
↑ Head north toward 39th St
56 ft
(I tell A. we are only going home to eat then we are going
bowling)
↑ Continue on to MacArthur BART Access Rd
272 ft

(We both say how sweet the air is)
(Shall we keep walking past home?)
⤶ Turn left onto 40th St
0.2 mi

(There is a flirtatious altercation between a woman

and a man that involves sudden running. I grip
A.'s arm instinctively. He reassures me)

➤ Turn right onto West St

0.3 mi

(We stop to smell some flowers)
(We are very much in love)

◄ Turn left onto 44th St

0.3 mi

(I remark blithely on the darkness and the lack of street-
lights A says something about the city council
and the budget)

985 44th St

Oakland, CA 94608

(I notice one jogger who turns out to be a fast runner)
(I notice another behind him—is there a fight?)
(I notice a third coming onto the pavement behind us)
(I understand that we are the prey. I prepare my hands
beneath my mouth
to catch my leaping heart)

These directions are for planning purposes only. You
may find that construction projects, traffic, weather, or
other events may cause conditions to differ from the map
results, and you should plan your route accordingly. You
must obey all signs or notices regarding your route.

Map data © 2019

Google

INCIDENT NUMBER:
█████████████/YOU

█████████████████ at approximately 2155 hrs he was walking █████████████████████████████████████

██

██

███████████████ heard footsteps ████████████
█████████████████████████ turned around and saw three
subjects ████████████████ S-1 ██ M █ 5'6–5'7,
years old, ████ complexion, wearing █████████████
████████ armed ██████████████████████████ S-2 ████
M █ 5'6–5'7, ████ years old, ████ complexion, wearing █
████████████████████████████████ S-3 ████
████ M █ 5'6–5'7, █████ years old, █████ complexion,
wearing ████████████████████████████████████
████ one of the subjects demanded ████████████
██████████████ their belongings. ██████████████
S-1 was holding a firearm ████████████████████
████████ he feared for his safety. ██████████████
██
S-2 and S-3 pushed ████████████████████ fall ████████
██
took ████████████████████████████████████
██
████████████████ then fled ████████████████

51

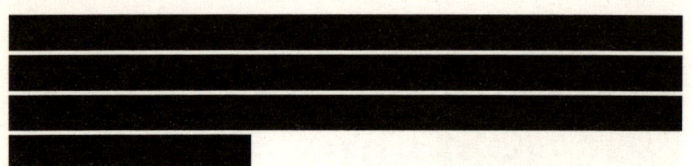

POLICE REPORT

44   the drowned boy

43   stretches for air

42   unpeels his fist

41   reveals it

40   fraught

39   with treasure

MULTIVERSE (I)

Awaiting CT results, we spend many hours meditating alternatives.

At first, they are sensible:

Q. What if we had gone bowling like I suggested?
A. we were hungry

Q. What if we hadn't taken that route?
A. would another have spared us?

Q. What if they'd waited ten seconds more and we were indoors?
A. they could have entered the house

Q. What if the neighbours with the mid-century furniture had come out twenty seconds earlier?
A. it happened quicker than we remember it

Q. What if the camera outside Chris' had recorded it?
A. he never signed up for the premium plan that records things

Q. Why didn't I fight harder?
A. you fought hard enough

INCIDENT NUMBER:
▓▓▓▓▓▓▓/ME

she could not breathe.

4TH MAY (PART ONE)

on the 2-train
a novel change

                                       hyper
                                 ventilation.

what if

      this   ends   this
      beat   instant?

that night

            I neglect
        the *Shahada*

              (yes; I believed
               we would die

              no; it didn't
              occur to me)

that night in

      all the things   I say
      all this is   to say

there is hostile *'ein*
on me.

                              Mama!
                    burn your *harmal*

          pop them all.

ANOTHER IMPORTANT LESSON IN PRIORITISATION

In Arabic: في مهم وفي أهم

That is to say: *there is that which is important, and that which is most important.*

> While I worry people envy me,
> it is important not to envy.

> This means: restraining my body.
> It craves a bite of every joyous family.
> Every good place. Every open arm.

4TH MAY (PART TWO)

Back

on the train
I am

perplexed.
Who is trapped

in clawed
windows?

It feels more true   more true

I am unable to dress
without gold.

Accounting for
time difference

it is not yet   one week
(I must still be in shock).

Nineteen years
(I carried
those things).

Breathed beside beating
chest closer

than

                    mother friends everything
                    I have loved.

There must be
some intermediary
between

                    people &
                    objects

or else

there must be
some conversation
since

        some   objects
        mean more than   people &

in some cases

        objects become
        living beings.

Like surrogates.

NOTE TO SELF

Every word and sentence I form, I want to note down.

If I repeat a thought or feeling to more than one person, it immediately becomes untrue.

Several descriptions feel that way since. My ordeal has become a script.

Sometimes I improvise, but mostly it's the same.
I modify the spectators.

When this happens, it feels cheap. As if I have made a performance of a trivial incident.

A performance of confession.

The first time I leaned forwards and did not feel the ritual swing of gold against the sink, I was terrified.

I know about phantom feelings: pain from limbs long gone. I say this to A., he understands and consoles me.

Every time I have invoked 'phantom pain' since, I have sullied myself.

Authentic pain can only happen one way, once, then.

Any more, and it is just imitation.

Must I find a new rawness for every retelling?

Although I have a lot of people, this shrinkage of language makes me feel very alone.

MULTIVERSE (II)

Later, they are repentant:

Q. What if I had not changed my flight and had gone back to New York the day before?

A. ...

Q. What if I hadn't shaken off my shame after our sweat that afternoon and had left the chain on the dresser?

A. ...

OUT OF BODY

Alone, you return
>everything now rotten
>the butter, the jam, the milk.

You see a hair, bleach the bathroom floor.

You sleep thirteen hours
>you worry flaked skin from your legs
>will taint fresh sheets.

You notice
>the food in the shops also rotten
>the fish, the beans, the oranges.

You forget an umbrella, become porous.

You walk at night, untroubled
>still, you fashion your water bottle as a club
>still, you start when your shadow bifurcates.

You put too much lemon on your food, by mistake
>your whole mouth, broken, burns
>for a short moment
>your sorrow dims.

SAFE

In Arabic, time is
a sword. Cut it or it
will cut you. But I think
time heals, if you also work
to heal. I think time is
dispassionate like that.

TALISMAN (5)

Other necklaces include:

a) زينب. My name; the way the Prophet said it. (05–19)

22ND MAY

Unexpectedly,

I feel

a remarkable

tranquillity

&

decide to go to Baghdad

if

my visa arrives.

I suspect

the gash running

down

my chest

will bleed

differently

will not

be noticed.

Because I am

anonymous

&
because
their
wounds
are

bigger and more.

I AM DREAMING ABOUT
THE APOCALYPSE

there is a road

at the border
we are told

stay

in the car
fallen from his fingers
the driver's ash
covers his knee

in our bag you will find:
two oranges
one bag of pistachios

good

many hours spent here
cars gathering, falling
like iron filings

The magnet is the crossing
The magnet is American khaki

after Maghrib, gunshots
a tap. Ablutions.
On leather, gauche prostrations

facing the wheel
spoken in zephyrs

'had I known you were British
I would have sold your names'

after 'Isha,
roving eyes
from reptilian tanks
(Al-Hamdulillah!)

It is time.
Tenderly unwrap red pamphlets
escort them from GMC to Humvee
a peace offering.

'We Will Protect the Brits'
(along with this believer
from Kentucky in his dishdasha)

In the belly of the compound (so secure! so warm!) we
have calculated: brown parcels of food + water + a doctor
+ a red plastic bracelet (= 'saved by grace').

'I wanna go to Piccadilly'
(of the private's eyes
only the whites animate)

Later, he is distressed
smudged as a bruise
'What? We shot him.'

                     Carried towards us:
              a dismembered nation

I am dreaming about the apocalypse
as a Westerner
only Whiteness helps you

forget

that the apocalypse
is simply a failed state.

THE MOST IMPORTANT LESSON IN PRIORITISATION

In Arabic: في مهم وفي أهم

That is to say: *there is that which is important, and that which is most important.*

This means: it is most important
to ignore

that a divergent path
could be possible.

'PATAPHYSICS

hayati
wake up!

that's enough now

the thing has happened
the magic has departed

as a baby
you lost a lot of gold
you lost a lot of gold

it never bothered me
with it went the envy

rather all of this
rather all of this

than the eye touch
even a hair

on our head.

TALISMAN (6)

Other necklaces:

a) Silver-ring on gold-chain. An Argentinian jeweller in Totnes. ('A placeholder'.) (15–19)

ELEGY FOR RETURN NO. 4

I am busy tonight. My love left a watermelon on my doorstep. It reminds me of rebellious women. Lining their roofs. Disobeying in RED WHITE GREEN BLACK. A fuck you. In America, fruit has no feeling, the black seeds bred out. Otherwise I would have dried, fried and salted them. Cracked them in displeasure. Left a trail of shells from A to B on the re-drawn map.

CROWN HEIGHTS/ UTICA AVENUE

In a moment/ of controlled clarity/ on the cusp of
'Eid/ and summer/ I recall/ what a friend tells me/
during those early/ dark months/ in America:/ Life is
continuum.

She explained it/ as a buoy/ out/ at sea/ bobbing/ in
concert / with water/ that shakes it./ Not immoveable/
but unmoved./ This/ then/ is just/ a nasty wave./
Calmer waters/ will come.

If I/ stay still.

ACKNOWLEDGEMENTS

Thank you, first, to my editors at Hajar Press, Farhaana and Brekhna, who believed in this book from the start.

Thank you to the Asian American Writers' Workshop and the Millay Colony for the Arts for trusting in me and supporting my work with time and community. Thanks especially to the wonderful women at AAWW: Jyothi Natarajan, Yasmin Majeed, Pik-Shuen Fung, Ayesha Raees and Jen Lue (whose tulips, in the days after my return to the city, brought me such serenity). Thank you to my Al-Shabaka family, for giving me space to write.

This book would be nothing without the generosity of Will Bordell, who showed me how to break poems apart and encouraged me to play with the pieces—thank you! And thank you to the many other friends who read or listened to versions of the manuscript over the years, particularly Tareq Baconi, Daniel Kelly, Nana Dakin, Katrina Ginis, Sean Wyer and Sarah Manchanda. Thank you to Ken Chen, for your literary guidance, and to Nyasha Weinberg, for your legal mind and your friendship.

To my Palestinian sisters, Nour Soubani, Randa Wahbe, Alia Al-Sabi, Bella Hammad and Yara Hawari—thank you for teaching me and growing with me. Thank you to Chris Yim for your loyalty and your astonishing capacity for introspection and to Libby Fitchett for your wisdom all those years ago. Thank you to the many more who have held and supported me across these many geographies.

My deepest love and thanks to my family—Mama (for everything, always), Khala Hanan and Baba. And to my chosen family—Genevieve Peattie, Hannah-Ida Azuonye, Anu Henriques and Natasha Rieffel.

Lastly, thank you, A., for protecting and loving me. For creating this universe together.